BY ALLAN MOREY

THE OAKLAND
RAIDERS
STORY

TORQUE™

BELLWETHER MEDIA · MINNEAPOLIS, MN

TM

Are you ready to take it to the extreme? Torque books thrust you into the action-packed world of sports, vehicles, mystery, and adventure. These books may include dirt, smoke, fire, and chilling tales. **WARNING**: read at your own risk.

This edition first published in 2017 by Bellwether Media, Inc.

No part of this publication may be reproduced in whole or in part without written permission of the publisher. For information regarding permission, write to Bellwether Media, Inc., Attention: Permissions Department, 5357 Penn Avenue South, Minneapolis, MN 55419.

Library of Congress Cataloging-in-Publication Data

Names: Morey, Allan, author.
Title: The Oakland Raiders Story / by Allan Morey.
Description: Minneapolis, MN : Bellwether Media, Inc., 2017. | Series:
    Torque: NFL Teams | Includes bibliographical references and index.
Identifiers: LCCN 2015047963 | ISBN 9781626173774 (hardcover : alk. paper)
Subjects: LCSH: Oakland Raiders (Football team)–History–Juvenile literature.
Classification: LCC GV956.024 M67 2017 | DDC 796.332/640979466–dc23
LC record available at http://lccn.loc.gov/2015047963

Printed in the United States of America, North Mankato, MN.

TABLE OF CONTENTS

TIED FOR FIRST ⎯⎯⎯⎯⎯⎯⎯⎯⎯⎯ 4

OUTLAWS OF THE NFL ⎯⎯⎯⎯⎯⎯ 8

THEN TO NOW ⎯⎯⎯⎯⎯⎯⎯⎯⎯ 14

RAIDERS TIMELINE ⎯⎯⎯⎯⎯⎯⎯ 18

TEAM SUPERSTARS ⎯⎯⎯⎯⎯⎯ 20

FANS AND TEAM CULTURE ⎯⎯⎯ 24

MORE ABOUT THE RAIDERS ⎯⎯ 28

GLOSSARY ⎯⎯⎯⎯⎯⎯⎯⎯⎯⎯ 30

TO LEARN MORE ⎯⎯⎯⎯⎯⎯⎯ 31

INDEX ⎯⎯⎯⎯⎯⎯⎯⎯⎯⎯⎯ 32

The Oakland Raiders face the Kansas City Chiefs on December 24, 2011. The game starts slow. The first half ends with a 3-to-3 tie.

Denarius Moore

The Raiders take the lead early in the
second half. **Quarterback** Carson Palmer
tosses a 61-yard bomb to **wide receiver**
Denarius Moore. Touchdown!

The fourth quarter ends like the first half, with a tie. The game goes into overtime.

The Raiders get the ball. Palmer tosses a long pass to receiver Darrius Heyward-Bey. This sets up a field goal. The Raiders win! They are now tied for the best record in their **division**.

Darrius
Heyward-Bey

SCORING TERMS

END ZONE

the area at each end of a
football field; a team scores by
entering the opponent's end zone
with the football.

EXTRA POINT

a score that occurs when a
kicker kicks the ball between the
opponent's goal posts after
a touchdown is scored; 1 point.

FIELD GOAL

a score that occurs when a
kicker kicks the ball between the
opponent's goal posts; 3 points.

SAFETY

a score that occurs when a player
on offense is tackled behind his
own goal line; 2 points for defense.

TOUCHDOWN

a score that occurs when a team
crosses into its opponent's end
zone with the football; 6 points.

TWO-POINT CONVERSION

a score that occurs when a team
crosses into its opponent's end
zone with the football after
scoring a touchdown; 2 points.

7

The Raiders are known as the **outlaws** of the National Football League (NFL). They have been known for a tough style of play. Longtime owner Al Davis liked his team to play rough.

Fans enjoy their team's **reputation**. They show it by going to games decked out in wild costumes.

Oakland, California, lies on the eastern shore of the San Francisco Bay. It is a busy port city.

The Raiders currently play home games at the Oakland Alameda **Coliseum**. This stadium is also home to baseball's Oakland Athletics. Each time the football field is changed to a baseball field, it costs $250,000!

OAKLAND ALAMEDA COLISEUM

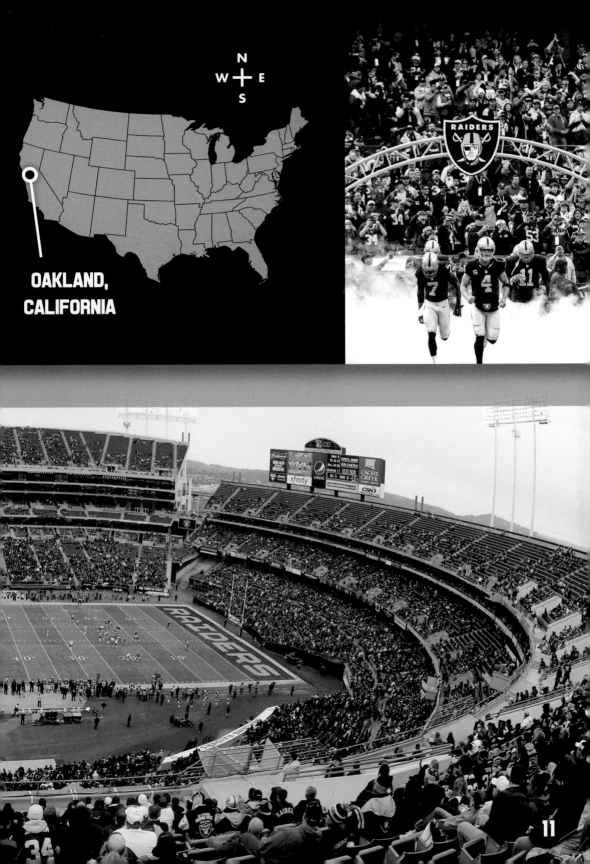

OAKLAND,
CALIFORNIA

The Raiders joined the NFL in 1970. They play in the American Football **Conference** (AFC). They are part of the West Division.

The West Division includes the Denver Broncos, Kansas City Chiefs, and San Diego Chargers. The Raiders' main **rivals** are the Broncos and the Chiefs. Many fans also feel a strong rivalry with the nearby San Francisco 49ers.

NFL DIVISIONS

AFC

AFC NORTH

BALTIMORE **RAVENS**

CINCINNATI **BENGALS**

CLEVELAND **BROWNS**

PITTSBURGH **STEELERS**

AFC EAST

BUFFALO **BILLS**

MIAMI **DOLPHINS**

NEW ENGLAND **PATRIOTS**

NEW YORK **JETS**

AFC SOUTH

HOUSTON **TEXANS**

INDIANAPOLIS **COLTS**

JACKSONVILLE **JAGUARS**

TENNESSEE **TITANS**

AFC WEST

DENVER **BRONCOS**

KANSAS CITY **CHIEFS**

OAKLAND **RAIDERS**

SAN DIEGO **CHARGERS**

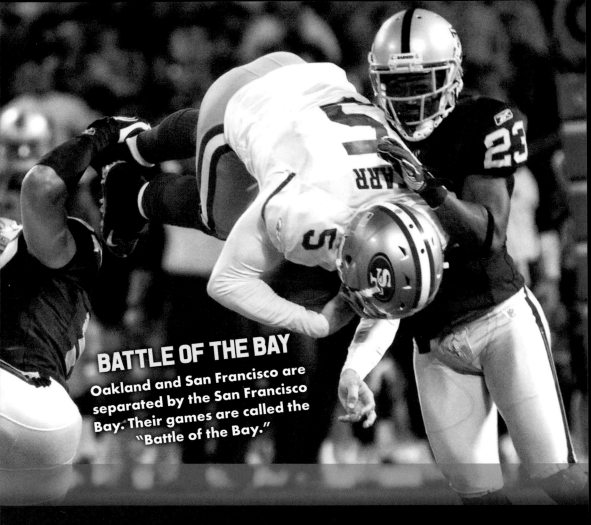

BATTLE OF THE BAY

Oakland and San Francisco are separated by the San Francisco Bay. Their games are called the "Battle of the Bay."

NFC

NFC NORTH

 CHICAGO
BEARS

 DETROIT
LIONS

 GREEN BAY
PACKERS

 MINNESOTA
VIKINGS

NFC EAST

DALLAS
COWBOYS

GIANTS

 PHILADELPHIA
EAGLES

WASHINGTON
REDSKINS

NFC SOUTH

FALCONS

CAROLINA
PANTHERS

 NEW ORLEANS
SAINTS

 **BUCCANEERS**

NFC WEST

CARDINALS

LOS ANGELES
RAMS

SAN FRANCISCO
49ERS

SEATTLE
SEAHAWKS

The Oakland Raiders almost did not exist. The American Football League (AFL) wanted a team in Minnesota. But in 1960, the NFL planned to put the Vikings there. The AFL awarded a team to Oakland instead.

JUST WIN
Al Davis coined the Raiders' team slogan, "Just win, baby!"

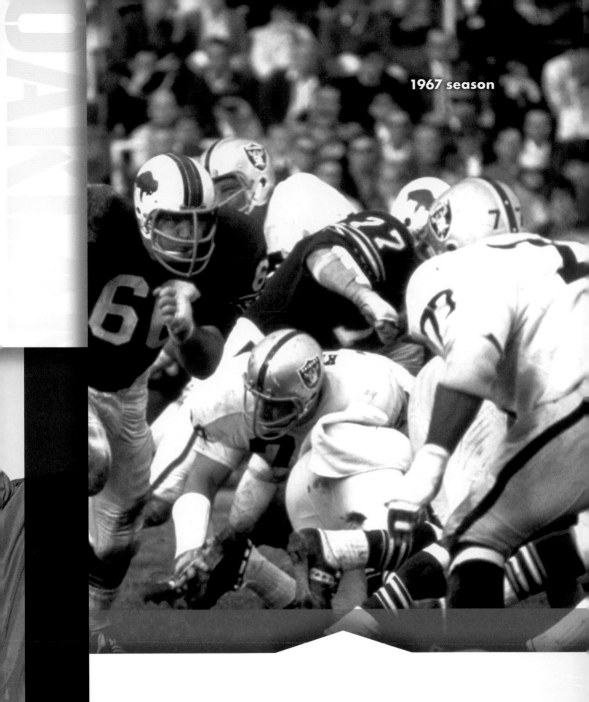

The Raiders struggled at first. They won only nine total games in their first three seasons.

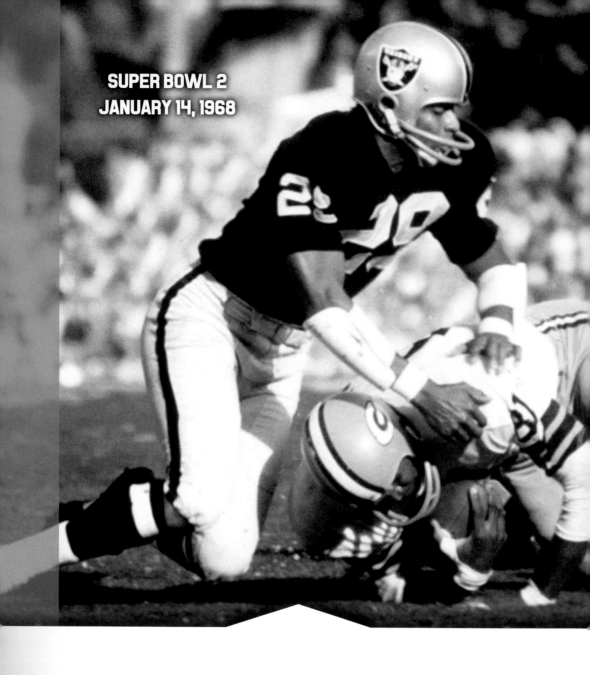

Things changed starting with the 1967 season. The Raiders made it to **Super Bowl** 2. They lost that game. But in the 1970s and 1980s, they won three Super Bowls!

After the 2002 season, the Raiders faced the Tampa Bay Buccaneers in Super Bowl 37. The Bucs were coached by Jon Gruden, the Raiders' former head coach.

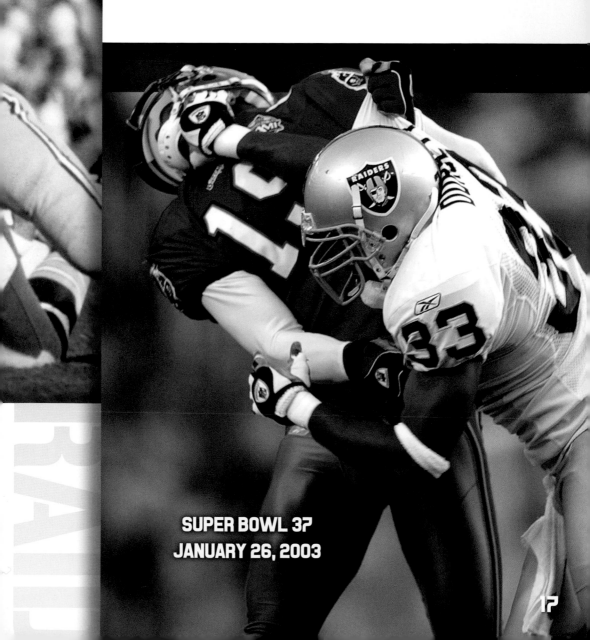

SUPER BOWL 37
JANUARY 26, 2003

RAIDERS TIMELINE

1960
Joined the AFL

1968
Played in Super Bowl 2, but lost to the Green Bay Packers

 14 **FINAL SCORE** 33

1977
Won Super Bowl 11, beating the Minnesota Vikings

 32 **FINAL SCORE** 14

1969
Hired coaching legend John Madden

1970
Joined the NFL

1981
Won Super Bowl 15, beating the Philadelphia Eagles

 27 **FINAL SCORE** 10

1982

Moved from Oakland, California, to Los Angeles, California

1984

Won Super Bowl 18, beating the Washington Redskins

38 FINAL SCORE **9**

2003

Played in Super Bowl 37, but lost to the Tampa Bay Buccaneers

21 FINAL SCORE **48**

1995

Returned to Oakland

2014

Drafted quarterback Derek Carr

Star **center** Jim Otto was one of the first Raiders. Gene Upshaw and Art Shell joined him in the late 1960s. They formed one of the best **offensive lines** in NFL history!

Jim Otto

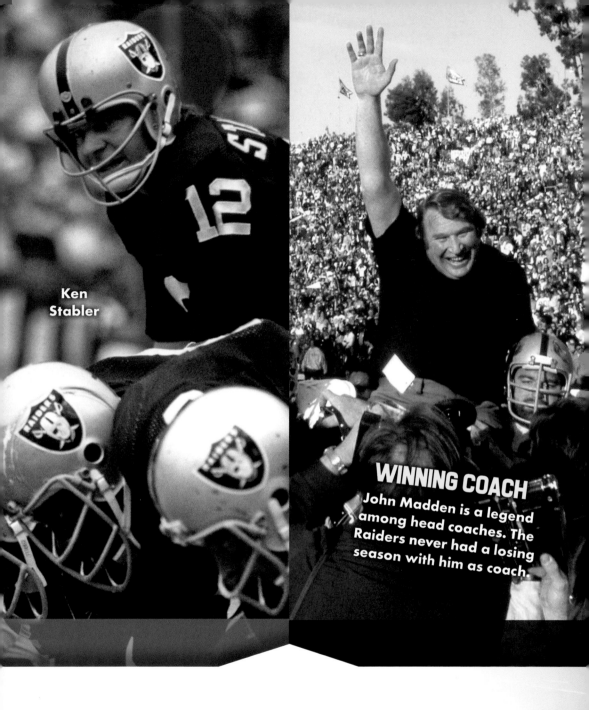

Ken
Stabler

WINNING COACH
John Madden is a legend
among head coaches. The
Raiders never had a losing
season with him as coach.

In the 1970s, quarterback Ken Stabler led the
Raiders to their first Super Bowl win. He remains
the team's all-time leading passer.

The Raiders' all-time leading **rusher** is Marcus Allen. He was the league's **Rookie** of the Year in 1982.

Defensive end Howie Long was another star in the 1980s. He was known for **sacking** opposing quarterbacks. Today, Khalil Mack is a sack leader for the Raiders.

TEAM GREATS

JIM OTTO
CENTER
1960-1974

GENE UPSHAW
GUARD
1967-1981

ART SHELL
TACKLE
1968-1982

Derek Carr

Amari Cooper

BUDDING STARS
Quarterback Derek Carr now leads the offense. Wide receiver Amari Cooper is one of his favorite targets.

Raiders fans act like their team. They are proud of being loud and wild. Fans from other teams see them as **villains**.

Dressing up in silver and black is a tradition. Each fan is creative with his or her look. Face paint, skulls, and spikes make many of the fans' costumes scary.

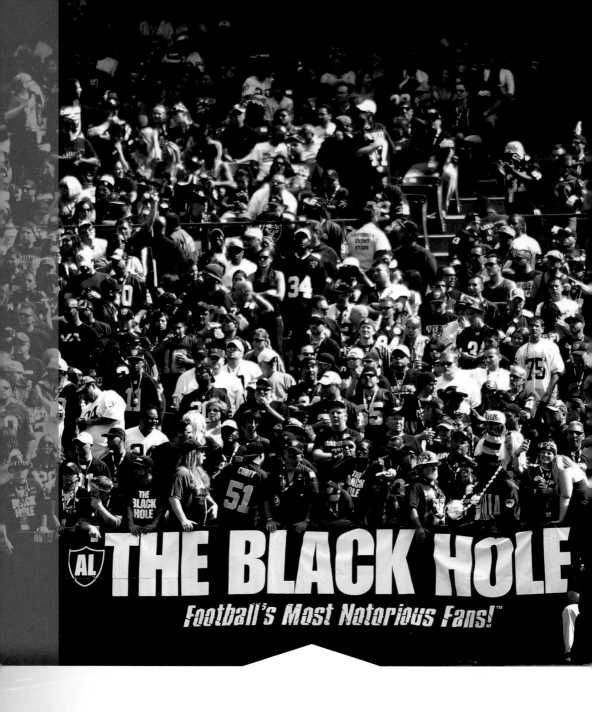

THE BLACK HOLE

Football's Most Notorious Fans!™

The Black Hole is the place in the Oakland Alameda Coliseum to avoid. It is located at the south end of the stadium.

The rudest and craziest fans sit there. They cheer on the Raiders and tease opposing teams. They lead the fans in pulling for the Raiders to claim the Super Bowl title once more!

MORE ABOUT THE
RAIDERS

Team name:
Oakland Raiders

Team name explained:
Named to sound tough;
the original team name,
the Señors, was weaker.

Nickname:
The Silver and Black

Joined NFL: 1970
(AFL from 1960-1969)

Conference: AFC

Division: West

Main rivals: Denver Broncos,
Kansas City Chiefs

Hometown:
Oakland, California

Training camp location: Napa Valley
Training Complex, Napa Valley, California

CALIFORNIA

OAKLAND

N
W + E
S

Home stadium name:
Oakland Alameda Coliseum

Stadium opened: 1966

Seats in stadium: 53,250

**Logo: A black shield
with the word RAIDERS,
crossed swords, and
a pirate wearing a
football helmet**

Colors: Silver and black

Name for fan base:
Raider Nation

GLOSSARY

center—a player on offense whose main jobs are to pass the ball to the quarterback at the start of each play and to block for the quarterback

coliseum—a large arena

conference—a large grouping of sports teams that often play one another

defensive end—a player on defense whose job is to tackle the player with the ball

division—a small grouping of sports teams that often play one another; usually there are several divisions of teams in a conference.

offensive lines—groups of players on offense whose main jobs are to protect the quarterback and to block for running backs

outlaws—people who break the law or other rules

quarterback—a player on offense whose main job is to throw and hand off the ball

reputation—the opinion people have about something or someone's character

rivals—teams that are long-standing opponents

rookie—a first-year player in a sports league

rusher—a player on offense who rushes with the ball

sacking—tackling the opposing quarterback for a loss of yards

Super Bowl—the championship game for the NFL

villains—bad guys

wide receiver—a player on offense whose main job is to catch passes from the quarterback

TO LEARN MORE

AT THE LIBRARY

Howell, Brian. *Oakland Raiders.* Mankato, Minn.: Child's World, 2015.

Kelley, K.C. *AFC West.* Mankato, Minn.: Child's World, 2012.

Wyner, Zach. *Oakland Raiders.* New York, N.Y.: AV2 by Weigl, 2015.

ON THE WEB

Learning more about the Oakland Raiders is as easy as 1, 2, 3.

1. Go to www.factsurfer.com.

2. Enter "Oakland Raiders" into the search box.

3. Click the "Surf" button and you will see a list of related web sites.

With factsurfer.com, finding more information is just a click away.

American Football League (AFL), 14, 28

award, 22

Black Hole, 26, 27

championship, 16, 17, 21, 27

colors, 25, 29

conference, 12, 13, 28

Davis, Al (owner), 8, 14

division, 6, 12, 13, 28

fans, 9, 12, 24, 25, 27, 29

Gruden, Jon (head coach), 17

logo, 29

Madden, John (head coach), 21

name, 28

nicknames, 8, 13, 28

Oakland Alameda Coliseum, 10, 26, 29

Oakland, California, 10, 11, 13, 14, 29

players, 5, 6, 7, 20, 21, 22, 23

positions, 5, 6, 20, 21, 22, 23

records, 21, 22

reputation, 8, 9, 24, 25, 26, 27

rivals, 4, 12, 13, 28

scoring terms, 5, 6, 7

Super Bowl, 16, 17, 21, 27

timeline, 18-19

traditions, 9, 24, 25, 26, 27

training camp, 29

vs. Kansas City Chiefs (December 24, 2011), 4-7